Hector

Poems by Chloe Cocking

Hector

© 2019 Chloe Cocking
ISBN: 978-1-927848-41-8
First Softcover Edition
Filidh Publishing, Victoria, British Columbia

Cover Design: Chloe Cocking
Cover Image: *"The Snake"*
is licensed under CC BY-ND 4.0
Read about the license at https://creativecommons.org/licenses/by-nd/4.0/legalcode

Do not reproduce by any means this book, or any portion thereof, without written permission of the publisher.

*For Rachel and Holly
Fight the power, girls.*

Hector

Table of Contents

(untitled 1)	1
Church Bell	2
STFU	3
I'm more than a little annoyed	4
Under the influence	5
on writing a poem	6
Waters	7
idiopathis uticarin	10
burning words	12
bored	15
hanged man	18
(untitled 2)	19
An Ellipse has Three Dots, Asshole	21
list of things not worth remembering	26
Not News	27
"The ocean's dark shoulders rise and fall all night"	33
Not Dead Yet	34
(untitled 3)	36
About the Author	37

Hector

Hector

*You will do foolish things,
but do them with enthusiasm*

~ Collette

(untitled 1)

common is not

never was   exactly
common

common is not the word we need

no word
i know for what i know we need

Church Bell

every thing outside
is trying to kill me
i said

nancy laughed
she thought i was kidding

her bare feet describing
gentle ovals
in river water
as clear and cold as
that church bell i heard in amsterdam
@ 5am

STFU

i all ways enter   talking[1]

now here come the clichés:

>gift of gab
>blabbermouth
>kissed the Blarney Stone[2]
>motor mouth
>Chatty Cathy[3]
>silver tongued devil

for some this is akin to a crime

not for me

---

[1] Not all poets are quiet. #notallpoets
[2] Why should talking be synonymous with lying?
[3] A childhood nickname and a macabre doll made in the 1960's, like me. Macabre. because dolls should BE QUIET.

i'm more than a little annoyed

i am arcing toward menopause
right at the time
various products for menstruation
have developed
past the point of
"let's just jam some cotton in there"

Under the Influence

perimenopause

the Playtex 18-hr bra w/ tru-support and comfort straps, model 4693

hangry

concern about exorcisms (there're on the increase)

post-it note addiction

dissatisfaction with art

gordon's ceramic glaze # 3 in bottle green & cobalt blue

glue (not sniffing it, using it to glue things to other things)

questions about the the lack of cell formation in my pour paintings (what's going on there lately?)

lust to solve problems (more of a problem than you might think)

on writing a poem

it seems like shit
some times

pernicious poison
twisting in a drainage basin
acid green spiral

the surface water lost underground

but
some times

it's beauty and rage

Waters

i. swimming pool

chemical birth-stew

it's not the chlorine that makes your eyes red
it's the attention of boys on your no-longer-flat
    chest
along with father's fists

girls whisper
side-eye over tuna sandwiches

ii. pond

auntie pat waved, meaning *come out, come out now*
i did

little girl body in a one piece
compact, dolphin-dense

there were leeches on my shins

auntie pat burned then with her menthol cigarette
'til their soft bodies curled and fell off

iii. lake

rolled off the air mattress
little girl log

i didn't know i was drowning
so cold my collarbones ached

bob up
take a breath
float down
            whisper a trail of bubbles

idiopathic uticaria

my head is always the last part of me that knows knowing starts elsewhere in the body

some things get caught in the net of language and others do not if i bat knowing away—like i usually do—it travels around my body

18 months of hives from my clavicle to the soles of my feet idiopathic uticaria an objection to a man i worked for

then he was fired, boiling in shame

worst part? i rode the elevator down with him as he left, trapped in a metal box with a predator

he lied + said he was going to buy his lunch in his eyes the scared lonely animal who had to go home and break it to his wife and child my heart full of agape love like they told me in sunday school so who is the real idiot here? why can't i simply hate assholes and be done with it?

my skin cleared up the next day

that wasn't the first time

i had hives 10 years before that raw red islands my body a fear-map charting topography of the most wicked kind of love like the past still too much the little girl who loved and hated in equal measure i thought for good reason i lived with a man with coward's fists and casual cruelty

(tho' not only those things if it matters probably not)

burning words

can't get the words out fast enough
feels like four brains instead of stomachs
but only one mouth

i know why cows moo
bellies churning with grass

my belly is full of burning words

some words are so stupid i can barely endure them
must cushion myself with incredulous quote marks
"moist"
"undulating"
"panties"

i never read pornography:
i fear some writer has written "moist, undulating panties[4]
that phrase is out there some where waiting circling overhead
if it lands in my ear
i might never be able to have sex again

my belly is full of burning words

---

[4] not sure what the phrase would signify; the mind boggles.

some are lemon drops
sweet n' sour, saliva squirting:
cute
tart
tang
tickle
tantalize

some are ridiculous:
hippopotamus
flabbergasted
ailurophile[5]
embrocation[6]
argle-bargle[7]

some hold troubled grace:
blossom
amnesia
butternut
lullaby
alcazar[8]

---

[5] Lover of cats.
[6] The application of lotion.
[7] Copious but meaningless talk or writing.
[8] A Moorish palace or fortress in Spain.

Hector

    some brim with mystery:
    mickle[9]
    abomasum[10]
    mistigris[11]
    famulous[12]

    these all burn my belly until i moo

---

[9] Very large.
[10] The fourth stomach of ruminant animals.
[11] The joker or blank playing card declared "wild" in a card game.
[12] Associate or assistant, esp. one who assists a magician or a scholar. Alas it does not apply to those who assist poets.

bored

i wonder how many stories i can write about parrots and decapitated heads before i'm bored?

j. irving wrote a lot about bears and sexual assault before he was done with those topics. w. shakespeare droned on about cross-dressing and mistaken identity, elizabethan theatre's just an extended three's company episode. i know, i know i'm not supposed to shit on shakespeare but how many times can a character say "that's can't possibly be him, that guy's wearing a different hat!" before credulity stretches itself thin as a.b.c.[13] gum?

anyway w. shakespeare is pushing up the daisies, j. irving is too, for all i know. besides, j. irving is only canonical to certain tweedy gents who wish they were still allowed to grope the undergrads in their am-lit seminars.

pro tip: don't have a 3-way with an am-lit professor and his ex-wife because afterwards at least one of them will tell you should read the novels of j.irving and like a dummy you'll think this is a

---

[13] "already been chewed".

good idea and go to the library and find the novels and wonder wtf is up with all the rape and all the bears.

but i digress: w. shakespeare and j. irving don't care what i think.

fine by me. in this we have some common ground. often i don't care what i think.

why should i? thoughts are like buses, wait ten minutes & another one comes.

even then, it might not be the thought you need—thoughts are tricky that way—so you might have to wait another ten minutes to catch the next thought, and then that one is no good either, like the last #14 hastings of the night, vomit pooling near the rear seats 'cos everyone's drunk, and either happy or unhappy, riding their own thoughts in their own ways. also fine by me. i get skeeved by the vomit, tbh. then again you have to meet people where they're at, there is no other option. plus who am i to judge bus-vomiters? i've thrown up in all kinds of inappropriate places, and it's only happenstance that it was never on the last #14 hastings of the night.

so they'll ride their thoughts and puke and be happy or unhappy, and meanwhile i'll keep on with the parrots and decapitated heads until i get bored.

hanged man

she used to dream of a hanged man

                face blue
                tongue swollen
                bent neck at an angle
                    horror & humour in
    equal parts

on bad days she saw him when she was awake
too eventually not

terrifying
or funny
any more

he was   just there

(untitled 2)

i looked for my courage i found none

can i stop?

                                              stop what?

this. i changed my mind

                                              the time to change your mind was nine months ago

i'm serious

i'm too scared

isn't there some drug . . .

(imagine a road work flagger

red lollipop reading stop!)

                                              nurse shook her head

                                              metronome of no

Hector

                                                not bloody
                                                likely, lady

i could stop just

for a little while

(voice wheedles like a chisel)

just until i'm ready

                                                your baby is
                                              ready
i imagined my baby   already

slippery naked fish

i imagined us both

trapped in ancient amber

An Ellipse has Three Dots, Asshole

in 1974

the journal of applied behavior analysis published

"the unsuccessful self-treatment of a case of 'writer's block' "

it contained a total of zero words

i'm not sure where i'm going with this . . .

b/c i can't be

b/c it is

not 1974

or 1984

or 1994

or even

1854, as so many,

it seems,

would like it

to be

        . . . except to say . . .

Hector

if it was that hard
to say what was
on your mind
or important
or urgent
or true
in 1974

it is more than hard now

b/c once the beast ate truth
greedy
it sucked down language, too

so it is
not just
the problem
l. anderson noticed
(that language
is a virus)

it is also
that in post-truth

        literally

nothing sensible

      . . . sensible in the sense of making sense . . .

can be said

or written

on the internet

or anywhere else

(is there any where

that is not the internet?)

so i

propose this

as a tool of resistance . . .

correct only grammar, spelling, and punctuation

some of this work

could be

delegated

to bots

no matter what

the words

arguments

communication platforms

"messaging"

or other bullshit term is trending right now

(i'm looking at you "disrupt", you traitorous motherfucker)

(also fuck the idea of "trending", while we're at it)

correct only grammar, spelling, and punctuation

teenage nazis tweeting about chugging milk?

correct their grammar, spelling, and punctuation

angry men shouting about lying bitches

ruining their reputations with accusations?

correct their grammar, spelling, and punctuation

politicians telling humans from illinois to

"go back to where you came from"?

correct their grammar, spelling, and punctuation

i doubt it

will do much more

than confuse them

                at first

even if bots help us

but

over time

and with consistency

i think their discourse will unravel at the seams

"everything is a weapon if you hold it right [14]

                                    ~ July 2019

---

[14] a. difranco.

list of things not worth remembering

what they said

how i felt

why i cried

that i cried (when do i not?)

how his hands looked

what i thought it meant

what i was afraid of

Not News

i.

where we are in this very moment

i'm confused why

there's so much confusion

and i wish i could help with your confusion but i too

am confused with your confusion as those

who are reading right now are also so so

confused but listen:

for the last two years we've all been confused

ii.

most have confusion about
the trump presidency
by his actions
in how he
has acted
so to see where we are at this
point right now
in and of itself is
striking and historic and maybe like a mamet play:
coffee is for closers
first prize is a cadilliac
second prize is a set of steak knives
third prize is you're fucking fired

iii.

this is one
of those moments where if you're in your
bed right now you're huddled around
your twitter feed and a bottle of wine and maybe a bag of   potato chips
saying oh my god the guy
he wants on SCOTUS
is a premeditated dude-bro gang rapist asshole
who knows no 'no'
can't believe that someone said no no no
i mean this is one of those aha moments

iv.

except the problem is
the whole presidency has been
one big aha moment for some it's hard
to grasp and understand what's happening
right now but people should be fully
aware of what's happening right now

v.

except the other problem is
that this has always been happening and i
for one, among millions,
knew that i was just meat
the first time my dad hit me so hard
there was blood on the wall
the first time i noticed men's heads
turning as they looked at my body
as i walked to elementary school
the first time a man told me he'd cut my little
   tits off
unless i was quiet and smiled::

i could go on but you get the idea

vi.

so what i'm confused about
is why anybody is confused about
knowing that no was not
needed or heeded
now
knowing no "no" ever mattered
knowing that no is not needed or heeded
   now
is not news, exactly

                                         ~ September 2018

**"The ocean's dark shoulders
rise and fall all night"**[15]

and so it is with love
prevailing or otherwise
a flow & ebb like breath

may be it's not enough

and some times
(forgive me)

it can be hard to care

what ever the end is
it will happen long after i'm gone
my children will be gone too
and they've had the good sense not to have
children

and yet
and yet

i'm still in love with the world
hoping for the best

---

[15] From Li-Young Lee's "The Undressing".

Not Dead Yet[16]

it starts with a twitch
big toe or left pinkie finger
round slumbering body of earth
re-covering from injuries

i say injuries when really i mean
devastation but i dislike that word
it blots out the light

after all
there is not just pavement
but also
        cracks
                in
                        pavement

if peace love and understanding
are broken + funny[17]
not monolith or behemoth
that is to say, not whole

the other side
horror cruelty and sadism
are not whole either

---

[16] Thank you, m python.
[17] I wonder about this alongside e costello.

which brings me to a fact:
animals live + plants grow near Chernobyl
may be ones you don't like
ones not what they would have other wise been
but there any way
the world has been
ending and beginning
since the beginning
and even if right now actually is
the beginning of the last ending

there will still be
anaerobic bacteria and
unfathomable lashings of time

(untitled 3)

somewhere a magnolia petal

(older than time-out-of-mind
one hundred and thirty million years or so
holy shit, right?)

**drifts to the dirty sidewalk below
the smokers**

(standing out side the bar
yakking enjoying a butt bitching about the live band)

don't notice

somewhere on mars, water

(too salty to freeze, crouches
two kilometers or so
beneath a solid ice vest
holy shit, right?)

may or may not be plump with life

~ July 2018

About the Author

Chloe Cocking is a writer and visual artist. She lives in New Westminster BC with her person and her cat. She is preoccupied with coffee and Japanese KitKats. Chloe can usually be found sitting on her living room floor surrounded by glue sticks and tiny little pieces of paper.

She is the author of *Blood Rain* (Filidh, 2017), an urban fantasy/horror novel, and *Fables Fictions and Fantasies: A Compendium* (Filidh,2018), a collection of weird, sad, and humorous short stories. If Chloe ever writes a memoir, she might call it *Weird, Sad, and Humorous: The Chloe Cocking Story*. That sums up life, right?

Hector is her first book of poetry.

Hector

www.ingramcontent.com/pod-product-compliance
Lightning Source LLC
Chambersburg PA
CBHW031437040426
42444CB00006B/861